INAUGURATION

OF

WASHINGTON UNIVERSITY

AT

SAINT LOUIS, MISSOURI.

APRIL 23, 1857.

BOSTON:
LITTLE, BROWN AND COMPANY.
ST. LOUIS: JOHN HALSALL AND COMPANY.
1857.

RIVERSIDE, CAMBRIDGE:
PRINTED BY H. O. HOUGHTON AND COMPANY.

CONTENTS.

EXERCISES IN THE MORNING AT ACADEMIC HALL.

EXERCISES IN THE AFTERNOON IN THE HALL OF THE MERCANTILE LIBRARY ASSOCIATION.

EXERCISES

AT

ACADEMIC HALL.

INTRODUCTORY REMARKS

BY REV. DR. ELIOT,

PRESIDENT OF THE CORPORATION.

FELLOW CITIZENS: With a degree of pleasure which I cannot adequately express, and with feelings of profound gratitude to Him without whose blessing none can thrive, I welcome you here this day, to take part in the Inaugural Exercises of Washington University. The work is indeed only begun, but the few steps of assured progress already taken justify us in large hopes for the future. Institution-building is and must be a slow work, and if at the end of twenty years we shall have succeeded in the full accomplishment of our plans, it will be a remarkable rapidity of growth.

The Act of Incorporation of this Institution, known at first as Eliot Seminary, was approved February 22, 1853. Its passage was obtained by the exertions of Hon. Wayman Crow, at that time Senator from this district, to whose feelings of personal friendship the name first selected must be attributed. As he was the sole originator of the design, and himself prepared the charter, the existence of the University is primarily due to him. No action under the charter was taken until February 22, 1854, at which time a full meeting of the corporators was held and the constitutional organization of the institution completed under the name of Washington Institute, afterwards changed to WASHINGTON UNIVERSITY, as now held. The incorporated name was also changed at the earliest day practicable, so that this is now both our legal and recognized title.

The charter under which we act is unexceptionable,—broad and comprehensive,—containing no limitation nor condition, except one introduced by our own request, as an amendment to the original act, namely, the prohibition of all sectarian and party tests and uses, in all departments of the institution, forever.*

The time has now arrived when we may, as we think, without arrogance, claim the right of being inaugurated,—to take a humble place, which we hope may become, in the course of years, an exalted place, among the Educational Institutions of the land. The sacred words of Scripture, which is the great underlying charter of education and civilization, of moral and intellectual growth and freedom, now forcibly suggest themselves to our minds: "Except the Lord build the house, they labor in vain who build it; except the Lord keep the city, the watchman waketh in vain."

The prayer of inauguration and dedication was then offered by Rev. TRUMAN M. POST, D.D.

* See Appendix, A.

ADDRESS OF J. D. LOW, A. M.

ADDRESS

By J. D. LOW, A.M.

PRINCIPAL OF THE ACADEMIC DEPARTMENT.

Mr. President: The occasion which we this day celebrate—the inauguration of Washington University, affords a befitting opportunity for those, to whose care you have committed the academic department, to give a brief explanation of the course of instruction which you have adopted, and which it has been our duty to put in practical operation.

In assuming the charge of an infant institution, whose future looks far down the vista of years, if we do not fully appreciate all the obligations and relations which this charge involves, yet permit me to assure you, in behalf of my associates, that we are deeply conscious that you have entrusted to us interests far more precious to you than silver or gold, yea, than all the "wealth of Ormus or of Ind."

I trust you will not understand me as assuming any great degree of merit in the humble sphere in which we labor, if I further state that we are almost painfully sensible that obligations are resting upon us, from which the boldest might shrink without the charge of cowardice; obligations, the performance or non-performance of which will find a culminating point, not in an hour, or in a day, but in the centuries beyond.

In establishing a course of instruction, it has been our aim, as far as possible, to combine practical and theoretical knowledge. We are aware, that in this practical, money-making age, many are solicitous for what is called a practical education; by which is meant, if we rightly understand the term, (of which we are not sure,) an education designed to fit us for the specific duties and callings of life.

We believe we fully appreciate the importance of practical knowledge; and it will be found that ample provision has been made in the different departments of the University, to satisfy every demand of the age; but we are well persuaded that education, to be thoroughly practical, must be founded upon an accurate knowledge of elements and principles.

With this in view, the first part of our course is necessary elementary—designed to be systematic, thorough, logical. The full Academic course embraces a period of eight years. Commencing with the child at the age of ten, it carries him through a series of years the most critical in human existence. During the first three years, the instruction will be confined to the simplest elements or rudiments of knowledge.

We are sure that we cannot assume an undue importance for this period of education. The soil of the youthful mind must be prepared and the seed sown with great care, if we hope to witness in after years a rich and generous fruitage. Success in the more advanced part of the course, will depend, in a great degree, upon the proper direction given to the youthful mind, as it enters upon the threshold of learning. Great care will therefore be taken, that the mind shall be kept active and expanding, ever opening to the reception of such elementary truths as will give vigor, without overburdening.

At the commencement of the course, the study of the German language will be entered upon; and after a suitable interval, the French language. We believe that these languages may be learned at a very early age. As soon as children begin to talk, they commence the acquisition of language. It is not necessary that it should be a grammatical exercise,—they may learn conversationally. This is our method at the outset; and when the mind is more mature, the grammatical structure may be taught.

The study of these important languages will be continued till the whole range of literature which they contain shall be open to the student.

The study of the English language will receive special attention. In the words of Fowler, "our language, as the depository of the wisdom and experience of past generations, we have received by inheritance, to be transmitted to the ages to come; certainly enlarged, and, if possible, improved. A man should venerate his native language as the first of his benefactors; as the awakener and stirrer of his spiritual thoughts, the form and mould and rule of his spiritual being; as the great bond and medium of intercourse between his fellows; as the mirror in which he sees his own nature, and without which he cannot commune even with himself; as the image by which the wisdom of God has chosen to reveal himself to him."

With some such view of its intrinsic merits, we propose to enter upon the study of our noble Anglo-Saxon tongue, and pursue it in some form, throughout the course.

As an auxiliary to the study of our own language, the ancient languages will hold no unimportant place. Latin will be commenced in the fourth, and Greek in the fifth year, and continued through the remaining part of the course. In teaching them, the system of double translation will be constantly brought into requisition. I do not propose, nor indeed is it suited at this time and place, to engage in the discussion of the mooted question as to the utility of the study of the classics. It may be sufficient to observe, that setting aside the great and positive assistance that would be secured in obtaining a critical knowledge of our language, we do not feel that we can afford to lose the mental discipline which this study assuredly imparts to the student. Our course in these languages will be found sufficiently extensive for the practical purposes of life or as preparatory for the University.

The study of history will extend through three years of the course. In this department the aim will not be so much to gain a knowledge of isolated facts, though this is not without importance, as to stimulate the pupil to reflection, reading, and inquiry. The possession of a knowledge of the past, with all its great revolutions, social, political, and moral, to every one who aspires to be considered well informed, is so apparent that I need not dwell on this topic.

Considering the intimate connection of the mathematics

with the mechanic arts, and the physical sciences, they must always hold an important place, if not the most important, in every course of instruction. As a means of mental discipline, no doubt they have been greatly overrated, but as the handmaid of the arts and sciences, as an auxiliary in aiding us to penetrate the arcana of nature, they have no rival, and demand our first consideration. Commencing with arithmetic and extending through the various branches of mathematics, our Academic course ends with the calculus. The instruction in this department will be rigidly exact and thorough. In the demonstration of principles, the pupil will be taught self-reliance, to depend upon himself and not upon the teacher.

While we shall aim to make thorough mathematicians, we do not desire them to be exclusively such, so that they can perceive no beauty and appreciate no excellence in any thing, unless it contains an angle or a demonstration. The exclamation of the mathematician, who arose from the reading of the sublime Milton, with What does it prove? we hope may find no response in the hearts of those who go forth from these walls. The man in whose breast no nobler emotion, no loftier patriotism arises, from the words that breathe, and thoughts that burn, of the noble band of orators and poets, of this and other lands, living and dead, whose genius has added lustre to the human race, is not, in the true sense of the term, educated.

I have alluded briefly, I fear far too briefly, to some of the prominent features of our course of instruction. I may not omit to mention mental and moral science, political economy, and other kindred branches as forming a part of our scheme, but time forbids that I should dwell upon them ; nor, indeed, is it necessary, as they are related in no remote degree to topics to which I have already alluded.

The Academical course is elementary and preparatory. We claim for it no more ; but such as it is, we hope it may open to inquiring minds the vast fields of knowledge which lie beyond. We trust it may prepare the student to enter with honor some other department of the University, and pursue more extensively some branches of study of which he may have had a foretaste, or to undertake the exploration of new and untried paths.

I will add a few words as to classification, methods of instruction, and government.

To each teacher is assigned a particular department of instruction. In this division of labor, regard has been paid to the peculiar qualifications of the teacher ; and his tastes have been consulted. The attention of the teacher is thus directed to a few branches of study in which, by specific preparation, he may become eminently qualified to impart instruction.

Again, for each teacher the number of pupils is limited to twenty-five ; a number sufficiently small to admit of that individual attention and special instruction which the peculiar temperament or mental condition of the pupil so often imperatively demands, thus combining in a large degree the advantages of private and public instruction. Another obvious advantage is, that the teacher is able to examine each pupil minutely upon the lesson assigned, and thus know with a great degree of accuracy the exact progress he is making. The pupil thus coming in contact daily with the teacher, will receive at every stage of his progress his attention and co-operation. It will be perceived, from what I have said, that thoroughness is especially aimed at. We desire, not so much that the pupil shall master the book, as the subject; not so much to learn many things, as to learn much.

We desire, in a very particular manner, to guard parents against false impressions in regard to the progress of their children. Real and apparent progress are not identical. The studying of so many books, or so many pages in a book, is no test of real progress. The pupil may be making, apparently, rapid progress, while he is absolutely acquiring habits of thought and study which will unfit him for any eminent place among his fellows; or his progress may be, apparently, slow, while at the same time he is steadily but surely gathering around him the armory which will enable him to meet, if not without difficulty, yet with resolute courage, every obstacle that may oppose his success.

It is the duty as well as the privilege of every parent to carefully scrutinize and know what his child is doing. In order to throw around the pupil every possible safeguard—to establish a medium of communication between teacher and parent, and to elicit the prompt and active co-operation of the parent with the teacher, a system of monthly reports has been adopted. We invite your careful attention to these reports. You will find them to be exact transcripts of the teachers' opinion of your child. You may learn from these reports whether he is regular and punctual in his attendance upon the duties of the school, of his deportment, and of his rank and standing in his class. If your son is improving his opportunities, the report will be to you a messenger of peace; but if, on the other hand, he is wasting his time, the report will be to you a notice of warning. Take heed to it, and let no time be lost in consulting with the teacher. By so doing, you may save yourself from a greater grief. In sending you these reports, we transfer to you a part of the responsibility which bears heavily upon us every day. You cannot avoid it. You may shrink from it, but you must, nevertheless, meet it. If the voice of warning shall ring about your ears monthly, and you listen not to it, upon you will rest the responsibility; no hoarse and angry note of accusation will disturb the teacher's conscience.

I have as yet said nothing of the moral influence of the school. I speak of it last, though in itself of the most vital importance. We this day invoke, with no sectarian feeling, but in a Catholic spirit, the sanctions of religion in the inauguration of our enterprise. In this most public and solemn manner, we acknowledge the foundation upon which we rest.

I believe that our own WEBSTER has said that Christianity is a part of the law of the land.

Indeed, so interwoven is Christianity with our whole social fabric, so intimately connected with our civilization, that we cannot sever it from our enterprise, which has for its object social progress, without inflicting vital injury upon it. The gift of a copy of the Holy Scriptures, by the pupils, to Washington University, meets with the hearty response: "We accept and reverently acknowledge daily its divine teachings."

ADDRESS OF HON. JOHN HOW.

ADDRESS.

Mr. President and Fellow Citizens: Acting on the suggestion made, that a few words from me, as President of the O'Fallon Polytechnic Institute, a department of the University inaugurated here to-day, explaining our objects, and the views we entertain in seeking to work under the charter of Washington University, I shall briefly offer such an explanation.

It had been for some years the wish of those connected with the industrial pursuits in this city to establish here an institute that would advance the interest of those connected with them. In seeking this object, their attention was attracted to the different institutions which were working for the same object in our country. With a few exceptions we found that the progress they had made, had not been what, in our opinion, it should have been. Our inquiries as to the cause of so little success, (not to say failure,) seemed to show, that the fault has been not in aiming at too much, but in aiming at too little. Content with establishing libraries, reading rooms, and the annual exhibition of manufactures, they rested from their labors; and arguing for the most part that in stopping here, they had gone as far as the mercantile classes had thought proper to go, forgetting the fact that for the most part our mercantile community had the advantages of better school education.

For, whatever is said of labor being honorable, most honorable, which certainly I shall not contradict, I err not in saying to you, that it seems to be the great desire of those who are educated, while they seek honorable pursuits, to escape from physical labor, however honorable it may be.

Our desire is to establish here in St. Louis an institution that shall have all the advantages of the mechanics' institutes of our country, with those of the polytechnic institutes of Berlin, Vienna, and other cities of Europe; to have a building where, besides the library, and reading-rooms usually found in the mechanics' institutes, will be found a place for the model of the inventor, with the engine to work it, and for a school of design. The professors of the various branches of science treat of the mechanic arts, and there are few of these arts which do not need, for their successful prosecution, a scientific education. Aware of the magnitude of our undertaking, we have therefore eagerly embraced the opportunity offered us here, by the opening of this UNIVERSITY, and have sought permission to work under its charter, believing that it presents to us the means for obtaining our object. Its professors will be ours, and by combining our energies, we shall be better able to remunerate them, and by so doing obtain a greater amount of talent.

The managers of the O'Fallon Polytechnic Institute believing that to be successful, they must commence with the young, have established evening schools, for the education of those who cannot have the opportunity of attending our free day-schools. The success that has attended them has been great indeed, having received, in the last three winters, near fourteen hundred scholars, whose ages average eighteen years. We also own in the University nine scholarships, seven of which are represented here. Our hall is not yet built, but we are full of hope, and there are those connected with its management who are not generally content with any thing short of complete success.

We have named our institute, for the purpose of identifying it with our city, after one, who, being a citizen of St. Louis, is not named last, in speaking of its advantages, and to whom she owes much of her prosperity. In the formation of our directory, we have not confined ourselves to those connected with manufacturing pursuits; we have called to our aid gentlemen connected with the different professions, as our co-laborers in this work, and as I trust one of those directors will follow me, I may well leave it to him to smooth off my sentences, and to fill any voids in my explanation of our design.

A few words in explanation of the advantages possessed in conjoining the different interests, if there are different interests, in its management. And here I will give the language of President Donaldson, the first President of the Philadelphia Franklin Institute—a man whose name should be spoken on all occasions of this kind—for not content with building up the Institution in his own city to a position second to none in this country, he has been always ready and anxious to aid in establishing others: "I ascribe our great success to the bringing to the side of the manufacturer and mechanic his professional brother." Said he to me, "Come to-night to our conversational meeting, and I will prove this to you better than by words." At that meeting, among manufacturers, were Sarchet the iron worker, Pat Lyon the fire-engine maker, Norris the locomotive builder, and among the professional men were Hare, Peat, Bache, and Brown. Models were exhibited and comment invited and freely offered. A blacksmith spoke of the difficulty of working his iron, and a suggestion was made to him of the cause, and a preventive thought of; a dyer, of the difficulty of combining certain colors, and a chemist, Prof. Hare, I think, explained to him the cause.

Acting in this way, we formed our directory, and with us it has worked well, and we expect to show those who may attend the commencements of this University some ten or twenty years hence, some of these lads before me, that will be a good commentary on the words I have spoken to you now.

ADDRESS OF HON. SAMUEL TREAT.

ADDRESS.

WITH a mind for weeks pre-occupied with other themes, I entered this hall a few moments ago, not expecting to take an active part in these exercises, but merely to listen to the anticipated addresses of others. Summoned thus unexpectedly, to speak in this presence, I am overwhelmed with so tumultuous a crowd of thoughts seeking utterance, that the difficulty is, not what shall I find to say, but what, with due regard to brevity, can I best leave unsaid.

The important point in our undertaking has now been reached when this young University is formally to take its place among the educational institutions of the age. At such a moment, without wandering in pleasing anticipations through the opening future, or pausing upon the imposing realities of the present, my mind reverts, involuntarily, to that "day of small beginnings," when, pursuant to the notice that they had been named by statute as corporators for the purpose, a few gentlemen attended a preliminary meeting in the parlor of one of our most honored citizens, to consider the propriety of a formal organization of the designated Board, so that, if afterwards it should seem advisable to move forward towards the founding of a Seminary of Learning, under the advantageous charter granted, its privileges might not be lost to the public.

With what distinctness, at this moment, the consultations of that hour well up in the memory!—the free interchange of views concerning the educational wants of the West and of the age,—the proper mode of giving force and living energy to the practical thoughts entertained,—the policy or impolicy of an early effort,—whence would come the necessary funds to place such an enterprise beyond the reach of failure,—the impropriety of any movement whose feeble and struggling steps might thereafter dishearten others,—the real character and scope of our colleges and universities, and their adaptation to the great work of a true American civilization,—the vast material resources of this Valley, with the varied and fast multiplying pursuits springing thus early into full and teeming activity,—the heterogeneous population, with all its diversified and seemingly conflicting habits and casts of thought, out of which is to come an unknown homogeneousness of life and society, leading to and defining a moral and mental order, the like of which, perhaps, has never yet been,—the present transition and plastic period, in which the formative process must go on, whether for good or ill, to be determined by the influences to which this age is to be subjected,—the never-waiting and ceaselessly surging, buoyant, reckless, indifferent spirit animating every phase of western life and passion, a seething caldron into which so many ingredients have been thrown, and into which each day dashes many still more incongruous, and the consequent necessity of some directing and re-creative power to preside over and give shape, beneficent vitality and healthfulness to the resulting compound;—the ill-guided efforts of uneducated labor in factories, workshops, mines, and counting-rooms,—also in our vast forests, on our inexhaustible prairies, along our mighty rivers, and over iron pathways of traffic and travel, with all the attendant waste of capital, toil, and living energies!—the stern and unbending realities of the moral and physical condition of the Great West,—the importunate demand that no time should be lost in applying the right plastic agencies, the illimitable and never-ceasing destinies that must hang upon the peculiar civilization which should, perchance, take permanent root in "this, the richest valley the sun in all his course looks down upon,"—all of these overpowering thoughts came into review, accompanied with prudential considerations of the feebleness of those assembled, of the limited means at their command, of the daily recurring pressure of their own private business, of their entire lack of strength, in time and funds, to grasp with requisite power the mighty industrial and intellectual forces which were sweeping the age onward with terrific and almost resistless energy to its unknown, yet predestined goal.

Few, if any, had entered that parlor with the expectation that more was then to be done, or even contemplated, than a formal organization under the charter—an organization to slumber on until favoring years or a happy concurrence of events should quicken its sleeping vitality into vigorous action. All were satisfied that an educational movement on a broader and more liberal basis ought soon to be made; and no one doubted that, when made, it should not be with a merely scholastic *curriculum*, but with a sweep so extended and practical as to embrace within its circle every department of intellectual culture, whether to be applied by the student in after-life, through some of the so called learned professions, or in the counting room or factory, or mechanic's shop, or on the decks of our large steamers, or down in the earth among its metaliferous veins, or in agricultural pursuits along the fruitful prairies, valleys, and hillsides of the West, or in making straight and secure iron pathways across a continent, or in exploring the unrevealed properties of the clod beneath his feet, or giving new application to the subtile and mystic powers yet hidden in the laboratories of nature. The whole circle of human knowledge is not too large for the pressing wants of this age, country, valley, or city. Hence the peculiarities and scope of our educational plan, resting largely, as yet, in earnest determination only, but ere many years, we trust, to receive a full outward expression.

Our first meeting did not lead, however, only to consultation. A few days had hardly passed before the large amount subscribed by some of those then present revealed that a conclusion had been reached, as to the immediate propriety of a direct beginning, of which others had not dared to hope. Still, the sum thus given, though unexpectedly large, was hardly adequate to a fit commencement of so broad a scheme.

At that moment, one of our fellow-citizens, whose name in this community is almost a synonym for generous and noble-hearted liberality whenever the public good demands a benefaction, and who, not then belonging to the Board of Directors, had chanced to hear of the embryo-plan—and whom I am rejoiced to see with us here at this hour, honoring the occasion with his ever-welcome presence—" sero in coelum redeat ! "—sent unostentatiously to the President title deeds to property valued now at more than sixty thousand dollars. From that hour, all chance of failure vanished.

That benefaction, coming as it did at the turning point in the enterprise, gave it the required firmness and certainty. What only a few evenings before no one had probably regarded, save as a good to be slowly and cautiously reached in the uncertain future, had most unexpectedly received vitality and proportions, demanding the commencement of the first edifice—that in which we are now assembled—preparatory to the organization of a corps of instruction.

Did time permit, it would be a pleasant duty to recount the various steps taken up to this hour—to recall the successive wants as they were suggested to the Board, and the generous donations from the few by whom they were promptly met,—the circumstances under which the educational corps was formed,—the serious deliberations upon the necessity of organizing, at the very start, the Scientific Department,—so as to meet what was deemed the most urgent of the educational wants of the West,—the alacrity with which those who had before contributed largely, added to their previous gifts, so as to accomplish that indispensable object,—and the zeal with which those selected as Professors and Teachers engaged in the work assigned them. But it would be indelicate, in this presence, to repeat the names and services of each of the benefactors and patrons and founders, although the temptation is almost too strong to be resisted. Some facts known to a few only, under the pledge of secrecy—which injunction cannot be disobeyed—must remain concealed until time reveals their worth.

The result, in part, is seen to-day. Around us are gathered nearly all whose donations in money and land and time and counsel, and whose unfaltering faith, have founded here, in the heart of this great Valley, (the destined home of more than a hundred millions of freemen,) an American University, on a plan as comprehensive as the educational wants of all classes and pursuits, and as liberal as freedom from partisanship of clans and sects, and as a true love for the universal laws of nature and of Nature's God, will permit; bearing, too, the name of him who to his country and age, and for all coming time, is the representative of the grandest human virtues.

As a director in the University, and as one of the managers of the Polytechnic Institute, I feel a double pride at this hour; knowing as I do how harmoniously they have hitherto worked together as parts of the same system, and how indissolubly they are interwoven for the attainment of the same great ends. Throughout the land there are scholastic institutions of great efficiency and high rank,—worthy of the profound regard with which they are cherished,—fountains whence flow, perennially, pure classic streams to beautify and improve American society. Long may they continue their blessed work!

The West has its due share of such institutions,—many, it is true, struggling, *longo intervallo* behind the honored shrines of Harvard, Yale, Union, Princeton, and Columbia. Some of the most far-sighted patrons of learning in the East, have felt the pressure of the times, and given new prominence to abstract and physical science, and especially to the applied sciences. Still much remains to be done, if old prejudices are to be finally exploded, and the controlling physical energies of a young and bounding nation are to be subjected to the directing power of a stronger and better culture.

There are more unwritten volumes of valuable information in the mart and workshop than have been gathered into our libraries. Men possessing that true learning, acquired by tradition, early training, or severe lessons of personal experience, are applying it daily, with the confidence which the unvarying relations of cause and effect should ever give ; acting upon and incessantly dealing with scientific principles, which have either found their way silently and unperceived from the laboratories or closets of the philosophers, or have been hit upon by some lucky accident after persevering experiments in the workshop, or by a chance stroke of some careless artisan, and which in their full force, and best applications, are yet wholly unknown to the pale student or learned professor. So, on the other hand, our library shelves are filled with books containing formulas and facts, which, if known to the artizan and agriculturist, would save months of useless toil, and a sad waste of misapplied capital. This busy, working-day world needs a more general diffusion of scientific truth ; and science itself needs more frequent contact with the useful arts. Each would, Anteus-like, rise from the contact with renewed vigor. Art has, by daily experiments, detected new combinations, and unthought of analyses, of which the philosopher remains profoundly ignorant. Many a student of nature has toiled fruitlessly in the endeavor to verify his most important discoveries, because ignorant of the simplest expedients to which manual skill and dexterity resort; and many an artizan has abandoned his best enterprises, weary and heart-sick at his great loss and the oft-repeated failure of his efforts, not knowing that his hand has been in repeated contact with, and just on the point of grasping, the very principle which, if seized, would have opened to him unbounded triumph, and untold wealth. It is time that this were otherwise—that theory and practice—science and art—walked ever, side by side, in the workshops of the city and the halls of philosophy. Each has lessons to teach, which the other needs to learn. The life-blood of science must quicken and invigorate the arts; and the arts should, in their turn, give new strength, useful hints, and fresh health to science. Such vigorous action and reaction ought to be incessant—an uninterrupted circulation of the life-blood maintained, from the heart to the head and hands and feet of the body politic, giving to the whole system a ruddier glow, quickening it by sympathetic action, and indicating the ever-reproductive power of Nature's laws, by which are to be created, in the distant future, "a new heavens and a new earth." In such a spirit the Institute is the industrial or practical department of this University—the department in which the professor and the artizan will meet with mutual benefit. Their treasured stores should not be concealed in libraries or workshops; each being most interested in learning precisely what the other best knows.

This department, as has just been said by its worthy President, has made a fair beginning, and is under the management of those, most of whom, like himself, from the workshops of the city, are never content with failure in any enterprise. It has commenced at the very foundation, by furnishing, through its evening school, to the apprentices and journeymen of the city, such facilities for education as they most need. It has opened the way to continuous study, by its library and by its provision for useful lectures hereafter.

In the future, it is hoped, that many of the students now before me, will, after having been thoroughly trained in every department of this University, take their appropriate places at the head of the industrial movements of the West,—the equals in every branch of knowledge, and in all respects, of the most learned and honored of the land.

When in the progress of the movements leading to the opening of the University, the corps of instructors had been organized, and this hall prepared for its students, the question arose whether the point had been yet reached at which a formal inauguration of the Institution should be held. As each director cast his eyes over the country in search of one who united in his own person all the qualities requisite for the occasion, and whose presence and words of wisdom would crown the enterprise with fresh hope, dispelling any lingering doubts of permanent success, all rested, instinctively and simultaneously, on the ripe scholar, patriot statesman, and gifted orator of New

England, who in response to the urgent request, is with us to-day, to aid in inaugurating here, in the centre of our common country, an institution whose influences, we trust, will be as wide as the republic of letters, as true as the laws of nature, as humanizing as mental culture, as pure as Christian morals, and as enduring as civilization. Surely, no place is more appropriate for such an enterprise; and none more gifted or worthy to give utterance to the thoughts of such an hour! I know that all are impatient for the moment to arrive—and none more so than myself—when from his lips we shall hear those eloquent utterances on which the great interest of this occasion hangs. It is therefore time for me to have done with this desultory talk—to leave you to the gifted voice and far-reaching thoughts of him who has honored his *Alma Mater*—Old Harvard—by filling the most exalted stations in her academic halls, and who has shed increased lustre upon our young Republic by serving her long and well at foreign courts, and in her halls of legislation, and at her cabinet councils,—whose ripe thoughts and profound views upon nearly every department of human culture and action have already taken their appropriate rank among the classic productions of the age.

REV. DR. POST'S ADDRESS.

ADDRESS.

I CANNOT forbear, under the impulse of the invitation so suddenly and so kindly extended to add my favoring voice to the present occasion, so far to respond as to express my earnest sympathy with the enterprise this day inaugurated, and my gratification at the favorable auspices under which it starts. I see around me, in the gifted and honored representatives of different classes and professions of my fellow-citizens here present, the assurance of much strength, and of general confidence in the movement; and my assurance of its success is greatly increased by the names that appear in its Board of Direction, and eminently by the well-known efficiency, and patient and successful energy of its President, so honorably connected with the origin of much that is good in this city, and under whose able management it has been conducted to its present position of promise.

I cannot forbear expressing my gratification in view of the fact that with so much strength of character, we have evidence before us this day, that much of the strength of wealth in our city is also rallying for its support, and that God has bestowed on those among us to whom He has given princely fortunes, a disposition to employ them for princely uses. I am glad to see them associating their names with institutions for popular education and liberal culture, that shall be their munificent and honorable monuments to a grateful Future.

I am sure I may add, among other glad and favoring omens of the present occasion, that one whose charm of eloquence has been so extensively associated with literature and culture in the East, is here to-day, to unite us by the bands of Beauty and Persuasion with our cousins and brothers on the Atlantic slope, in the assurance of their sympathy in our enterprise to accomplish here, beyond the Father of Waters, a work such as our common Fathers wrought on the shores of the great ocean.

It seems to me also to augur, or at least to merit success for the Institution inaugurated, that, while it is in especial sympathy with the masses, and aims to bless Labor with culture, and unite in happy combination the speculative and scientific with the great practical issues of popular education, it is also placed on a broad and liberal basis on which men of different ecclesiastical or political schools can labor together. Such joint action for a noble object is, through its unitive influence, a public benefit as well as an augury of success.

But though the Institution is by its charter pledged to be unpartisan and unsectarian, God forbid it should ever be unpatriotic or unchristian. And I am happy to believe there is a common ground on which, though with different partisan and ecclesiastic names and symbols, we can stand together in the great work of national education, without compromising or discarding those great and vital truths and principles, religious and political, which must constitute the ultimate warp and woof of all valuable culture and character. The tendency among us unquestionably has been too much toward division and subdivision in educational enterprises; until society is resolved into fragments so minute that hardly any one is strong enough to establish for itself a respectable system of institutions.

I am far from affirming that institutions distinctively ecclesiastic have not place and position, and are not doing a great and good work in American society. But while experiments are being made all around us, of institutions of that description, I am gratified to see in our young city an effort of such promise to establish a University on a catholic and general basis, on which fellow-citizens whose walk in life may be in other respects somewhat different, can unite. I believe such an institution has at this epoch in our history, a great, a good, a necessary work to do. Should this enterprise succeed as it promises, we may regard it as in some measure inaugurative of a new educational era among us; and while abstinent from some aims commonly, and perhaps beneficently associated with denominational institutions, we hope it may still be an accepted and a permanent instrument of effective service, not only in the cause of liberal culture, but also in the kingdom of our God, to whom we would this day dedicate it.

An Address was also given by the Hon. Edward Bates, in his own peculiarly felicitous manner, but unfortunately no report or copy of it could be obtained. The assemblage then adjourned to the Mercantile Library Hall, to hear, at 3 P. M., Mr. Everett's Discourse.

EXERCISES IN THE HALL

OF THE

MERCANTILE LIBRARY ASSOCIATION.

REMARKS

BY REV. DR. ELIOT,

PRESIDENT OF THE CORPORATION.

FELLOW CITIZENS: The Inaugural Exercises of WASHINGTON UNIVERSITY, having been commenced this morning at the University building known as "Academic Hall," will be now continued by an Address from our distinguished guest, whom you are undoubtedly impatient to hear. I share in your impatience, but the necessity is imposed upon me of detaining you, less than ten minutes, that the occasion on which we now meet may be understood. For WASHINGTON UNIVERSITY is of so recent date and so little known, that many of those here present might reasonably be held excused if they now hear of it for the first time.

It was incorporated four years ago, with a different name, the continuance of which might have given it a local and sectional character, and which was therefore changed by those most interested in the enterprise. But, under a happy coincidence, the charter had been "approved" on the 22d February, 1853, and the first meeting of the corporators, at which the organization of the Institution was accomplished, was held on the 22d February, 1854. By this coincidence of birth, the name of WASHINGTON UNIVERSITY was suggested. It is also a name admirably adapted to the plan proposed, namely, the establishment of an American University, upon the broad foundation of Republican and Christian principles free from the trammels of sect and party; a University for the people, whom WASHINGTON served; to educate the rising generations in that love of country and of our whole country, which the Farewell Address of WASHINGTON inculcates, and in that faithfulness to God and Truth which made WASHINGTON great.

The Institution comprises several *Departments*, and is intended to embrace the whole range of University studies, except theological, and to afford opportunity of complete preparation for every pursuit of practical and scientific life. Three Departments have been already established and organized,—the Academic, the Scientific, and the Practical (or Industrial) Departments; and others will be added as circumstances permit,—among which I would expressly name a Department of Law, and a Department of the Fine Arts.

For the present use of the academic and scientific department, a building has been erected on Seventeenth Street with ample room for the accommodation of two hundred and fifty students, and where *one hundred* are now in daily attendance. A large lot of land, containing four acres in "Beaumont Addition," has also been purchased for the future erection of University buildings.

A Chemical Laboratory, on the same lot with "Academic Hall," is nearly finished, and arrangements have been made for its thorough and complete furnishing, so that on the opening of the next term, in September, the best advantages of instruction can be supplied. A Scientific Library and some expensive apparatus are yet needed, but I hope will soon be obtained. In this connection, let me say that a superior Equatorial Telescope is now in the hands of the manufacturer, by order of our fellow-citizen, JAMES E. YEATMAN, at the cost of $1,500, for the use of the University.

A Collegiate Department has not yet been separately organized, except by the appointment of Professor, TRUMAN M. POST, to the Chair of History.

In the Scientific Department, the Chair of Mathematics and Civil Engineering is occupied by Professor JOSEPH J. REYNOLDS; that of Chemistry by Prof. A. LITTON; that of Comparative Anatomy by Prof. CHARLES A. POPE; and that of Botany and Natural History, by Prof. GEORGE ENGELMANN, now in Europe.

Of the Practical Department, which is a novel and important feature of the University, a few words must be said. It was a part of the original design in obtaining a charter, and its organization preceded that of the other departments, having been rendered feasible by a liberal endowment in land, now worth at least $60,000, by Col. JOHN O'FALLON, and of $20,000 in money by other friends; and, although yet in its infancy, it has already accomplished great good. For the first year, it was under the sole management of the Directors of the University, and nothing was done except the successful establishment of an Evening School for young men, the purchase of a Philosophical Apparatus and a course of Scientific Lectures. As the plan developed itself, it was thought best that this department, although continuing under the same charter, as a department of the University, should be placed under distinct management and control.

From its connection with the Academic and Scientific Department, it derives great advantages by the facilities afforded for a thorough education, by the services of an able corps of teachers and professors, by access to the Chemical Laboratory, and in many other ways—all of which will be enjoyed, so far as practicable, without charge, or at reduced cost. But all details of management and proceeding of whatever kind, are better attended to by a separate Board to whose hands the Department has been intrusted, under the title of "The O'Fallon Polytechnic Institute."

For its permanent and successful establishment, the one great desideratum now is, a large and convenient building, without which comparatively little can be done. I am, therefore, the more happy in announcing that I am authorized here to state, that, if a suitable lot of ground can be obtained for $30,000, it will be purchased and given by a friend of the Institution. *I am not authorized* to say, but assume the privilege and honor of saying, that the generous donor is one who has already contributed largely to our funds—a man whom this city has more than once delighted to honor —one of our mechanic princes, JOHN HOW.

I have been further authorized, since I came here to-day, by our largest benefactor, to say, that he will place at our disposal property, which at its lowest present valuation is worth $27,000, and which we propose to increase to the sum of Fifty Thousand Dollars, at least, as a fund for general University uses.

These noble gifts, together with other resources, will enable the University to enter upon its second academic year, free of debt, and with property, all of which has been contributed in the course of *three years*, of more than $200,000. The endowments of professorships, (except of one,) and a general productive endowment for University uses, are yet to be obtained, except as above indicated.

In conclusion, let me add, that the members of the corporation are conscious of no private or party purposes to serve. They have undertaken to establish, upon a broad American foundation, an institution of learning, practical science, and art; and under the blessing of God, *nothing shall divert them from their purpose.*

With this view, they have invited for this inaugural occasion, a national man, whom I now have the honor of again introducing to you; one who needs no title or office to distinguish him, who belongs not to one State but to the Union of States—EDWARD EVERETT of America.

ACADEMICAL EDUCATION.

AN ADDRESS

DELIVERED AT ST. LOUIS, 22d APRIL, 1857,

AT THE

INAUGURATION OF WASHINGTON UNIVERSITY

OF THE

STATE OF MISSOURI.

BY

EDWARD EVERETT.

TO THE

REV. DR. WILLIAM G. ELIOT, PRESIDENT,

AND TO

MESSRS. JAMES H. LUCAS, JOHN HOW, WAYMAN CROW, JOHN M. KRUM, SAMUEL TREAT, JOHN O'FALLON, JAMES SMITH, SETH A. RANLETT, CHARLES A. POPE, JOHN CAVENDER, N. J. EATON, PHOCION R. McCREERY, GEORGE PARTRIDGE, HUDSON E. BRIDGE, SAMUEL RUSSELL, THOMAS T. GAUTT,

DIRECTORS OF

WASHINGTON UNIVERSITY,

OF THE

STATE OF MISSOURI,

THIS DISCOURSE,

PRONOUNCED AT THEIR INVITATION, AND IN THEIR PRESENCE, IS, WITH THE BEST WISHES THAT THE INSTITUTION MAY PROVE A RICH BLESSING TO THE NOBLE VALLEY IN WHICH IT IS ESTABLISHED, RESPECTFULLY DEDICATED BY

EDWARD EVERETT.

Medford, Mass.
24th July, 1857.

ADDRESS.

I APPEAR before you, fellow-citizens of St. Louis, at the earnest request of the Trustees of Washington University of the State of Missouri. The respect justly due to an invitation from such a source, and a lively interest, ever cherished, in the cause of education, united with a strong desire to see this mighty West, and to salute the Father of her Waters, from one of the great centres of her rapid growth and power, have induced me, at considerable sacrifice of personal convenience, to undertake my present visit to your hospitable city. It has already been a source to me of the highest gratification. I feel as if my conceptions of our common country had, in a brief space of time, been mightily enlarged. It is, of course, impossible to form an adequate idea of an extensive region, so distinctly in any other way, as by traversing it, and inspecting it in person. We may read the most minute descriptions ; we may add up columns of statistical figures ; we may get the boundaries and the list of counties by heart in manuals of geography ; we may have at our fingers' ends tables of population, of the productions of the mine, the forest, and the field, of the number of natives and the number of foreigners, and of the children between four and sixteen ; but all this minute knowledge, though useful in its place, does not give a vivid idea of an immensely extensive and rapidly growing country. It is only when on board one of these floating palaces, we have stretched along the sea-shore, or traversed the sound, the river, the lake ;—or, mounted on the fiery wheels of steam, have rushed through winding valley and mountain gorge; crossing ridge after ridge, and stream after stream; counting our progress by degrees of latitude and longitude; passing from tier to tier of prosperous States; from rivers that roll into the Atlantic amidst the icebergs of Labrador, to those which pour their steaming floods into the Gulf of Mexico ;—it is only after this actual traverse and survey of the mighty region,—its cities, its towns, its hamlets; its boundless extent, its infinite variety of field, and mountain, and flood; its wide range of climate and of production,—natural and artificial, the work of Providence and man ;—the whole joyous and all but bewildering scene animated with its swarming millions, that we can fully understand the natural features, the vast improvements, the rapid progress, the impending future of the Union.

I experience a difficulty, my friends, in attempting to do justice to my feelings, as I find myself in the centre of that ancient province of Louisiana, the proudest memorial of the name of Louis XIV.; on the banks of the river which bore for a short time the name of his illustrious minister, Colbert; but a few miles below its confluence with the still mightier Missouri, which forms, with its tributaries, one of the most extensive natural systems of internal communication in the world; and within the precincts of the prosperous city, to which the enterprising adventurers of the last century gave the name of the military saint of France. It is on these vast and expressive natural pages, as well as in the learned tomes of our libraries, that the most instructive lessons of history are recorded. Louis the XIV., the most ambitious, the most magnificent, for a time the most prosperous, the most liberal, the most arrogant, and at length the most unfortunate of princes that have died on the throne, had two ministers,—Colbert and Louvois,—the good and evil spirits of his reign,—angels of light and darkness to him and his royal fortunes. The one stimulated his unchastened ambition with perpetual schemes of conquest; the other brought order out of the chaos of his finances, and established the industrial arts in his wasted kingdom. The one raised armies, built fortresses, and fanned the flames of his wrath against his feeble neighbors; the other sought to persuade him to found a solid glory on the welfare and affection of his subjects. Louvois poured his relentless hosts upon the Netherlands and wrapped the Palatinate in flames, where the memory of Louis, after five generations, is still execrated. Colbert, not content with all his efforts to improve the internal condition of France, sent forth the devoted pioneers of the Christian faith and culture to the new world, and stamped his master's name on the then imperial wilderness. As early as 1673, Father Marquette descended the Mississippi from the Wisconsin to the Arkansas; and ten years later,—just a century and three quarters ago the present year,—the heroic and indomitable LaSalle, in a frail bark of his own construction, accompanied with a few gallant spirits attempered like his own, not forgetting the singular attendance of "twenty Indians from New England," starting from Chicago, crossed the State of Illinois, passed the mouth of the Missouri and the Ohio, and,—first of civilized men, as far as our accounts can be relied on,—descended the noble stream to its mouth. There, on the 9th of April, 1682, he took formal possession, in the name of his sovereign, of the entire region drained by the mighty river which he had traced from its upper waters; and confirmed to it, if he did not first bestow upon it, the name of Louisiana. The Mississippi, as I have already observed, had borne for a short time the name of Colbert; but a wiser instinct soon restored to it the native appellation, and by that venerable name it will roll to the ocean, till the language we speak shall cease from the tongues of men.

That year, 1682, may well be marked in the annals of America; great starting-points in our history cluster round the date. In that year, William Penn landed on the banks of the Delaware. In that year, Josiah Franklin, a poor nonconformist English dyer, emigrated to Boston, and in one century afterwards, the youngest of his ten sons, Benjamin, signed at Versailles the provisional treaty which established the independence of the United States. The struggle between liberty and prerogative, which ended in the American Revolution, commenced in that year in New England; * and in that year LaSalle traversed the interior of the continent, from the mouth of the St. Lawrence to the Gulf of Mexico. As I go back in imagination from the prosperous days in

* Minot's History of Massachusetts, Vol. I. p. 51.

which we live to the date of these early adventures; as I trace in retrospection the history of the country from its one and thirty States; its twenty-eight millions of population; its thousand prosperous cities, its towns and villages innumerable, bound together in a great political confederacy which belts the continent; its commercial tonnage already the largest which the ocean bears on its bosom; its network of railways and canals, not inferior to that of the most powerful States in Europe; the innumerable steamers that crowd its interior waters; the immense contributions which it pours into the general markets of the world; its churches, colleges, and schools, and all the countless institutions in which Christian charity gathers the orphan families of want to her maternal arms; in a word, this world of physical, intellectual, and moral resource, development, and action; —when from this magnificent contemplation I retrace the line of history through the vicissitudes of policy and war, from the Union to the Confederation, from the Confederation to the Revolution, from the Revolution to the yet acquiescent state of provincial allegiance, and backward to the feeble youth and dependent infancy of the colonies; when I see how steadily, as I pass onward from generation to generation, this exuberant contemporary greatness converges and shrinks up into a narrow strip of provinces along the coast, a few small ill-built towns on the sea-side and the great rivers, some hundreds of straggling cabins on the western slope of the Alleghanies,—not one subject to English jurisdiction west of the Ohio and Mississippi a hundred years ago,—a half a dozen block houses and Missionary stations belonging to France, in the seventeenth century, beyond those frontier streams,—a border ringing with the war-whoop and gleaming with the scalping-knife,—great solitary rivers, as yet without a name or a burden, hurrying with idle lapse to the sea; and at last the awful silence of the eternal forest;—I feel as if I were following the Father of Waters from its mouth back to its source; tracing it from its emporiums of the world's commerce on the seaboard, between populous states, and beneath the walls of towering cities, leaving successively its grand tributaries right and left; upward and backward from the alluvial delta to the pleasant vicissitude of hill and valley; ranging with its parallel winrows of driftwood in great bends through broad zones of latitude and longitude; now tumbling for miles over broken ledges, and anon bursting through basaltic gateways, or sweeping across rolling prairies; from climate to climate; from the burning tropic back to the arctic glacier; from the land where the sultry breeze is scented with the orange and the myrtle, up to the region where the hemlock and the pine defy the northern blast; turning the flank of mountain ridges and making deep cuts through central plateaus,—narrower, shallower, purer as you ascend,—a gentle current, a rippling stream, a purling brook, a silver thread;—till at last all that is left of the mighty river, whose stupendous floods at its mouth wage equal war with the stormy ocean gulfs, lies sparkling in a cool moss-covered spring, fed by the trickling dews of the morning, enamelled with Alpine flowers, in the bosom of the lonely hills.

These reflections, my friends, are not only preliminary

to the remarks which you expect from me on this occasion, but are intended by me to strike the keynote of my address. We are assembled here, at one of the *foci* of this great western world, to inaugurate an institution for the highest departments of education; and you have invited me, a citizen from one of the extreme corners of the continent, to join you on this interesting occasion. Born and bred within the sound of the eternal roar of the Atlantic, upon the very spot where the foundations of my native State were laid two centuries and a quarter ago,—a region already presenting many of the characters of an ancient settlement,—a territory stripped of the native forest, a dense population, institutions venerable for their age and the traditions of the olden times,—you have invited me to meet you on the banks of this mighty inland river, whose very existence was but vaguely conjectured, whose extent and course were wholly unknown, when the settlements of New England commenced; and where the teeming life and vigorous progress of which so many manifestations surround us, are the growth of two generations, I had almost said of one; and my errand is to unite the expression of my good wishes and cordial sympathies with yours, on the steps you are taking to found a seat of liberal and practical education, adapted to the progressive character of the age, and the peculiar wants of the West. In approaching the subject, my thoughts involuntarily revert to the period to which I have alluded; and I feel more deeply than ever before, that there is nothing in human history which can compare in interest with the condition of the American continent on the eve of its discovery and colonization, and its transition into the sphere of civilized and Christian culture, looking back from our present point of view upon the various stages of this transition, as one great operation in the order of Providence.

Consider it a moment; there it lay upon the surface of the globe, a hemisphere unknown to the rest of the world, in all its vast extent, with all its boundless undeveloped resources, not seen as yet by the eye of civilized men, unpossessed but by the simple children of the forest. There stretched the iron chain of its mountain barriers, not yet the boundary of political communities; there rolled its mighty rivers unprofitably to the sea; there spread out the measureless but as yet wasteful fertility of its uncultivated fields; there towered the gloomy majesty of its unsubdued primeval forests; there glittered in the secret caves of the earth the priceless treasures of its unsunned gold; and more than all that pertains to material wealth, there existed the undeveloped capacity of a hundred embryo States; of an imperial confederacy of republics, the future abode of intelligent millions, unrevealed as yet to the "earnest" but unconscious "expectation" of the elder families of man, darkly hid by the impenetrable veil of waters. There is to my mind an overwhelming sadness in this long insulation of America from the brotherhood of humanity, not inappropriately reflected in the melancholy expression of the native races. The boldest keels of Phenicia and Carthage had not approached its shores. From the footsteps of the ancient nations along the highways of time and fortune,—the embattled millions of the old Asiatic despotisms, the iron phalanx of Macedonia, the living crushing machinery of the Roman legion, which ground the world to powder,—the heavy tramp of barbarous nations from "the populous north;" not the faintest echo had aroused the slumbering west in the cradle of her existence. Not a thrill of sympathy had shot across the Atlantic from the heroic adventure, the intellectual and artistic vitality, the convulsive struggles for freedom, the calamitous downfalls of empire, and the strange new regenerations which fill the pages of ancient and mediæval history. Alike when the Oriental myriads, Assyrian, Chaldean, Median, Persian, Bactrian, from the snows of Syria to the Gulf of Ormus, from the Halys to the Indus, poured like a deluge upon Greece, and beat themselves to idle foam on the sea-girt rock of Salamis and the lowly plain of Marathon; when all the kingdoms of the earth went down with her own liberties, in Rome's imperial Maelstrom of blood and fire,—and when the banded powers of the west, beneath the ensign of the cross,—as the pendulum of conquest swung backward,—marched in scarcely intermitted procession for three centuries to the subjugation of Palestine,—the American continent lay undiscovered, lonely, and waste. That mighty action and reaction upon each other of Europe and America,—the grand systole and diastole of the heart of the nations,—and which now constitutes so much of the organized life of both, had not yet begun to pulsate. The unconscious child and heir of the ages lay, wrapped in the mantle of futurity, upon the broad and nurturing bosom of Divine Providence, and slumbered serenely, like the infant of Danae, through the storms of fifty centuries.

But we should omit a most important link in the chain of reflection, by which I desire to illustrate the agency of educated mind in promoting the civilization of this continent, if we forbear to state that it was not wholly destitute of occupants of the same blood as those who from the creation of the world have performed the great drama of Asiatic and European life. These vast plains, though uncultivated, these forests which never rang to the music of the settler's axe, these lovely valleys which as yet wasted their sweetness on the desert air, were not wholly untenanted. They were the abodes of numerous tribes of our fellow-men, nowhere consolidated into powerful empires, at least not in this part of the country, though possessing in the aggregate formidable powers both of aggressive and defensive action ; a most interesting branch of the human family, whose condition, as far back as we can trace it, presents some of the most difficult problems in the history of our race. Gathered by the elementary instincts of our nature into rude social and political relations ; not destitute of a certain imperfect mental culture, which found expression in the pictured rhetoric, the wailing poesy, and the wild mythology of these blighted races ; speaking languages of a highly artificial and complicated structure, but wholly ignorant of that divine art, by which the creations of thought are embodied in visible signs and transmitted to other times ; from ages immemorial the vagrant lords of the soil, and for an unknown lapse of time undisturbed in its possession by violence from abroad ; a wandering but not a nomadic race ; owning no flocks nor herds but those which, with each returning spring, the Great Shepherd leads forth, in multitudes which darken the prairies, from New Mexico to Hudson's Bay; destitute of all the institutions and fixtures of a stable society; divided into rival communities, but instead of rising to higher stages of progress, in the lapse of time, by the emulations of peace or the collisions of war, rendered apparently from age to age more and more barbarous and degenerate, in the effect of their hereditary and internecine tribal hostilities;—producing chieftains of no ordinary capacity, such as King Philip of Mount Hope in the seventeenth century, Pontiac in the eighteenth, and Tecumseh in our day, all of whom conceived large designs but formed no systematic polity; acquiring no arts but those necessary for the chase and their stealthy murderous tactics; their senses trained, in the pursuit of their game or the enemy, to a preternatural quickness, which, however, admitted no intellectual or artistic application to the higher ends of life; they plainly showed, in the whole tenor of their history, that whatever may have been the mysterious design of Providence in placing them upon our continent, it certainly was not "to replenish the earth and subdue it," to develop its resources, to cultivate its wastes, and to make it the abode of civilized and enlightened races. That great work, experience has shown, was to be performed by another branch of the human family, whose advent, establishment, and progress on the continent of America have unhappily kept pace with the retirement and decline of the primitive inhabitants.

There is, in my opinion, no inquiry more profoundly interesting than that which regards the means and the agencies by which this great work has thus far been effected; by which, in not more than two centuries and a half from the first efforts at settlement, so much of our continent has been brought within the domain of civilization, and raised to so high a point of improvement in the arts of life and in intellectual culture; and this inquiry, if I mistake not, conducts us directly to the objects and purposes which have brought us together at this time; I mean to the subject of education, in the largest comprehension of the term. The immediate agencies by which the great work has been accomplished, the second causes, if I may so call them, of the rapid progress made in the civilization of the North American continent, are to be sought, no doubt, in various geographical, political, and moral conditions which it would require a minute and protracted analysis to trace in detail; but the great master cause, humanly speaking, the *causa causans*, is unquestionably to be found in the creative power, the resistless energy, and the legitimate sway of *educated mind*, acting upon this broad theatre, upon the inexhaustible materials of social improvement presented by the new found hemisphere, and working under the lead of a gracious Providence toward the elevation of our common humanity.

This great human miracle, I say, is the work of educated mind; and when you found a seminary of learning, you do but seek the farther development, discipline, and application of that ethereal power, which brooded over the dark chaos of the barbarism that covered our beloved America three centuries ago, bade light to shine upon its broad surface, set the great luminaries of intellectual and moral culture in its firmament, and called its lovely creations of art and knowledge, to life and day.

It is not brute force, nor material elements, nor political influences by which, in the last analysis, this all-important work has been achieved; it is the sovereign power of educated mind.

It would be foreign to my present purpose, though a most interesting subject of discussion, to trace to their sources in Europe the intellectual energies and influences by which this great work thus far has been achieved. It may be sufficient to remark in general that the first European settlers of this continent brought with them, in various measures, the intellectual culture of the old world, some in a high degree, a majority that portion which falls to the average lot of the mass of the community, and which places the day-laborer of Europe and America,—who reads a good newspaper week-days, and goes to church on Sundays,—in many respects on a higher level of intelligence, than the Sultan of Turkey, or the Shah of Persia. Assuming the seventeenth century as the period of colonization, the first settlers of North America left their native countries in the age of Bacon, and Shakespeare, and Milton, and Newton; of Grotius, of Pascal, of Descartes, of Bossuet, of Corneille, of Racine, of Galileo, of Tasso, of Kepler;—not to speak of other names, not unworthy to be mentioned with these, in preceding generations. They accordingly left the old world at a time, when cultivated mind had, in some departments, reached its culminating point. To prevent this intellectual culture from being extinguished, under the hard material conditions of the new world, was their earliest care. They immediately made such provision for education as circumstances admitted, in their new homes. Those whose means permitted it, and who desired greater advantages of education than the new settlements could furnish, were sent to European seminaries. Of whatever national origin the settlers might be—English, French, German,—a living cord of sympathy bound them to the cultivated mind of some one of the most improved peoples and languages of Europe. Geographically they might be the neighbors of the savage on the remotest frontier; the log cabin, with the green twigs sprouting upon it, might be their only shelter, and the wolf might howl by night at their threshold; but they were educated in the communion of the choicest spirits of our race, and every ship that crossed the Atlantic kept their minds in the neighborhood of the cultivated intellect of Europe. The young consumptive clergyman, who in 1637 just landing on the continent, on his way to heaven, laid the foundations of Harvard College, in Cambridge, brought with him, besides a pretty substantial ballast of dogmatic theology, some of the great masters of ancient wisdom, and that golden volume of Lord Bacon's Essays, of which it has lately been said, that "of all the productions of the English language it contains the most matter in the fewest words." * Franklin, a poor apprentice boy in Boston, picked up an odd volume of the Spectator, then lately published, and there learned his unaffected, transparent, English style; and the immortal young surveyor of Virginia, while living with Lord Fairfax, in the valley of the Shenandoah, then the very frontier of civilization, gave his leisure hours to the same inimitable pages.

* Quarterly Review, September, 1856.

In addition to direct literary culture brought from Europe, or kept up by constant intercourse with it, the multiform traditions of social life trained the masses. The great professional institutions of the old world were substantially transferred to the new. They carried to the remotest cabin of the settler of English descent, those foundation principles of social right which had been maturing in the common law for ages. The French settler brought with him the still older principles transmitted in the Roman code, from the most highly developed jurisprudence of the ancient world. The German emigration was of a later date; and its educated men, magistrates and preachers, had been trained in the intellectual system and habits of the most philosophical and speculative of the modern nations. Accordingly, although there was, for more than a century and a half, a hard struggle with material nature, and the political straights of colonial infancy, there was no disconnection from the mind of the civilized world;—no intellectual crudeness in any period of our history. Every thing which pertained to outward condition was rough, provisional, and imperfect; but high literary culture was perpetuated; and whenever grave counsel was to be taken, or important business transacted, or the written or spoken word to be employed in any branch of the public service, an astonishing ripeness and skill never failed to be disclosed. In this way, as a handful of disciplined soldiers, wielding the arms of civilized warfare, and led by intrepid chiefs, seldom if ever fails to triumph over any number of plumed savages; so the intellect of the European settlers, fortified with all the agencies of education, gained an easy mastery over the physical hardships that awaited them here; and operating upon this almost boundless field, comparatively safe from the political complications of the old world, has produced and is daily producing results, which, with all their familiarity, fill us with amazement.

To train and strengthen by discipline the powers of the mind, in other words to give still greater force and wiser direction to those intellectual energies, which have established civilized man in this western world, is the great object of institutions of education, from the humblest infant school to the most advanced seminary of learning, of science, of art, of the professions. Justly tracing their prosperity to its rightful source, plainly discerning a trophy to the triumphs of education in every square league of territory wrested from the wilderness, the people of the United States, in every stage of their progress, as far as local circumstances have permitted, have acted upon these principles, and have cared for education. They have regarded it, not as a separate interest of a favored class, but as the most important concernment of the whole community, practically interwoven with its inmost life.

From the early legislation of the colony of Massachusetts Bay which provided for the foundation of a college, and the establishment of a school in every town, down to the congressional reservation of one thirty-sixth part of the public domain for this purpose, more, I think, has been done for education in this country, and at an earlier period, by systematic public action, than under any other government. Nor, considering the comparative want of vast private fortunes in the new world, is the extent to which individual liberality has been bestowed in this direction less creditable to the country.

It may seem, therefore, a work of supererogation, in this country, on any occasion, or in any place, to attempt an argument on the importance of institutions of education; more especially on an occasion like this, which evinces in its very nature that you, at least, need no argument on the subject; and that, by whomsoever else or wheresoever else the duty of founding and endowing places of education may be called in question, it will not be done by those I have now the honor to address.

But though the universal mind of America has accepted as an axiom in social economy, that the largest possible provision is to be made for public education, it is perhaps rather in reference to elementary education in common schools that this principle has been established; and we frequently hear the necessity, sometimes the value of education as obtained in the higher institutions,—colleges, universities, and professional schools,—seriously questioned; and brilliant examples of "self-taught" men ominously and triumphantly quoted, to prove the inutility, if not even the inexpediency of academical training.

Nothing could be more abhorrent to my feelings than to speak disparagingly of self-taught men. I have neglected no fitting opportunity to eulogize them among the departed, nor to manifest sympathy and respect for them among the living. I know of no spectacle on earth, pertaining to intellectual culture, more interesting than that of a noble mind, struggling against the obstacles thrown by adverse fortune in the way of its early improvement; no triumph more glorious than that which so often rewards these heroic exertions. It is because I appreciate the severity of the struggle, and deeply sympathize with those who have forced their way to eminence, in the face of poverty, friendless obscurity, distance from all the facilities for improvement, and inability to command their time, that I would multiply the means of education, and bring them into as many districts of the country, and as near the homes of as large a portion of the population as possible, in order to spare to the largest number of gifted minds, the bitter experience by which those who succeed in doing so are compelled to force their way to distinction.

This premised, I have four words to say concerning self-taught men. The first is, that while a few minds of a very high order rise superior to the want of early opportunities, with the mass of men, that want, where it exists, can never be fully repaired. In the next place, although it is given to a few very superior intellects to rise to eminence without opportunities for early education, it by no means follows that, even in their case, such opportunities would not have been highly beneficial, in smoothing the arduous path and leading to an earlier and more perfect development of the mental powers. Accordingly we find in the third place, that highly intelligent men, who have felt the want of early education themselves, are (without an exception, as far as my observation has gone) the best friends of academic education; as if determined that others should enjoy the advantages of which they were deprived. It would not be necessary to leave this platform, to find the most striking illustrations of the truth of this remark. Lastly, this epithet, "self-taught," is subject itself to great misconception. It is by no means to be supposed, because eminent men, in any department of science or art, passed their first years and earned their first laurels without early opportunities of education, that they remained, more than other men, destitute to the end of their lives of instruction from abroad. Far otherwise; in all ordinary cases, the epithet in question applies only, with real significance, to the early stages of a distinguished career. As soon as a gifted person, however destitute of early culture, has possessed himself of the keys of science and literature, and gained access to books, he is no longer self-taught, he is a regularly entered pupil in the great high-school of recorded knowledge, in which the wise and famous of every age are the masters. He may have acquired the elements of any branch of literature or science by weary and solitary toil over the poorest manuals, but as soon as they are acquired, Euclid and Newton become his teachers in geometry; Addison and Goldsmith correct his compositions; Tully and Demosthenes teach him to speak. He learns his chemistry from Lavoisier and Davy; his electricity from Franklin and Volta; Galileo and Herschel teach him to point his telescope to the heavens; Thucydides and Tacitus are his lecturers in history; and Milton and Dante, and Virgil and Homer, conduct him to the inmost shrine of the muses; while, to encourage his progress by living examples,—not to mention the illustrious names of foreign lands,—he will find guides and models in every department of knowledge in his own country.

But there is an impression, I grant, perhaps a growing impression, on the part of a considerable portion of the community, that some at least of the studies pursued at our colleges and universities, as at present constituted, are scholastic, antiquated, and abstract; tending at best to the acquisition of learning which is rather curious than useful, and not adapted to qualify men for the actual duties of life.

Before inquiring whether this impression is well-founded, or attempting to meet the reproach which is implied in it, let me say a few words, if I dare do so in this utilitarian age, for the noble inutility of generous studies; rather let me call it for the ineffable beauty, dignity, loveliness, and priceless worth of the meditations and exercises of the thoughtful, well-instructed mind, soaring on the wings of its conscious,—nay, better, of its unconscious powers and susceptibilities,—far above the region of utilitarian appliances, to the highest heaven of thought, imagination, and taste. I am not so preposterous as to disparage utility, properly understood and pursued, but it is in its ordinary acceptation the handmaid of imperfection and frailty, and carries with it a greasy feel of selfishness,—a brassy taste of self. It implies wants to be relieved and defects to be supplied; hunger to be fed, nakedness to be clothed, and sheltered, and warmed; and the dependent weakness of a feeble and suffering nature to be armed against the thousand ills that flesh is heir to. And so with immense toil,—evil at once and remedy,—intense labor to obviate the necessity of laboring,—incessant care to gain relief from care,—a killing strain upon the faculties to procure repose of mind,—it plies the axe in the primeval forest, ploughs, and plants, and reaps the field, bridges the river, navigates the ocean, unlocks the gates of mountain chains, explores with groaning enginery the Tartarean depth of mines; drags up spouting Leviathan from the abyss; lifts from the earth, to warm and light our dwellings, great black clods, into which the forests of an elder world have been crushed and condensed; imprisons the mutinous force of steam in iron cells, there to work the bidding of its master; turns brawling rivers upon the wheels of industry; smelts the ore; poises the trip-hammer; forges the anchor; tempers the watch-spring; tips the gold pen with a spark of iridium; touches the needle with magnetic life; stamps thought upon paper; delineates the human face by the solar ray; packs up the ship's longitude in a watch-case; balances the steerage of tall navies on the gimbals of the compass-box; and transmits intelligence by the electric spark from continent to continent, beneath the ocean's bed. All this is the work of mind indeed; but of mind dealing with material forces and elements, to supply the wants and avert the sufferings of our physical nature; often, in the individual case, at the cost of greater hardships than it relieves. Man prays to Heaven for his daily bread. Heaven showers down no manna upon the waste, but teaches, through the inventive faculties, those bread-giving arts, and clothes the land with plenty.

But, oh, my friends, there is that in the capacities of our minds which is more than useful, and which deals with higher elements than those of material well being. It is not appointed to man to live by bread alone, and

> "The thirst that from the soul doth spring,
> Demands a drink divine."

There are facts in this great and wondrous universe, which it is delightful to trace, though we cannot as yet discern their relations to the service of man. There are truths and groups of truths, which seem to bind all creation,—the flower of the field, the stars of the sky, and the marvellous frame of man in bonds of strange analogy,—of which it lifts the soul from earth to heaven to catch a glimpse, as of a golden thread woven in the great loom of Providence through the mystic tissue of the Universe. Immeasurably above all the delights of sense is the serene rapture of meditation, the calm ecstasy of pure thought, sounding the depths of its own consciousness, and ruling all else which is subject to man, in the heaven above and the earth beneath, with the sovereign mastery of mind. Unspeakable are the attractions of patient enthusiastic science, now following the traces of creative wisdom, along the minutest fibres of microscopic life, and now clinging to the folds of the streaming robe of Omnipotence, as it floats over the transcendent galaxies of the highest heavens. Calm and pure the satisfactions of the scholar, who, aloof from the competitions and the prizes, the mean jealousies, the hollow pretences, the brutal vilifyings, the base intrigues, the measureless corruptions of public life, holds converse in his inoffensive seclusion with the unenvious wise and gifted of every country and every age. Exquisite the enjoyments of a refined taste, keenly alive to the beauties of sight and sound; to the fair creations which rival nature on the glowing canvas, or which start from the quarried marble, clothed with form and grace, beneath the sculptor's hand. Sweet the entrancement of music, as it breathes in vocal melodies from tuneful lips; or cries with almost human pathos from the chorded viol; or stirs the blood in the inmost chambers of the heart with the voice of the crashing trumpet; or rises and swells, and rolls, soft or loud, in full diapason, along the quivering arches of some grand cathedral, heaving and mounting in one overflowing tide of harmony from all the full-mouthed stops of the pealing organ far up to the resounding dome, and bathing in rich floods of music the resplendent forms of saints and martyrs, whose purple robes and golden halos blaze from the storied windows on high. And nobler, purer, higher than the inarticulate voice of chord, or reed, or flute, or sounding key, the articulate voice of Poetry; the music of the genius, the fancy, the heart; the nearest approach of the human faculties to raptures more than human; the earthly transfiguration of wisdom into prophecy, of genius into inspiration, of Nature into the supernatural, of the letter which killeth into the spirit which maketh alive; the brightest vision which mortal eye can catch of harmonies and relations beyond the pale of sense; the noblest conquest of humanity over time and fortune; mysterious quintessence of our intellectual being; the golden casket in which memory locks up her choicest treasures; the eternal column on which Fame records her brightest and dearest names.

But let us admit, for the sake of argument, that it is the business of places of education, not to train the mind to these higher tastes or minister to their gratification, but to pursue those studies and form those mental habits which tend directly to the practical uses of life, and, I think, we may still boldly venture to submit the usual branches of Academic learning to this test. I apprehend that we shall find that the value and importance of collegiate education can be sufficiently vindicated as the appropriate discipline and preparation for many of the most important departments of public and professional duty; understanding, when we speak of "the practical uses of life," not the life of a cabbage or a dray-horse, of "Epicurus' stye" or the anchorite's cell, but the life of a Christian man in civilized society.

It will be observed that I speak of collegiate education chiefly as a discipline and a training; not as if it dismissed its subject with an absolute fitness for the duties of life. The truth is, that education of all kinds, in many respects, begins precisely when in common parlance it is said to be completed. With the single exception of the languages,—if even they form an exception,—the absolute attainments to be made in three or four years passed at college, compared with those of after-life, are of minor consequence; especially when we remember how many departments of science and literature are in their nature so rapidly progressive, that theories which commanded universal assent thirty years ago, are now in many cases exploded, with every probability that another generation will work the same change with some of those which we adopt. But, while the law of progress thus operates on results,—habits of philosophical, cautious, and liberal investigation, formed in early life, will never cease to guide the conscientious inquirer to the discovery and application of truth.

It is, I know, a common prejudice against places of academical education that they must be comparatively useless, because they are stationary while every thing else is progressive. Universities have been wittily compared to vessels at anchor in the stream of time, serving little purpose but to show with what rapidity independent Research moves down the current. Many illustrious examples might be gathered from Academical history,—the names of Copernicus, and Galileo, and Newton alone are enough, as far as science is concerned, to refute this sarcasm. But, whatever may have been the case in former times, I think it can truly be said that nothing in Science, Literature, or Art is more progressive, at the present day, than Education in all its forms, Elementary, Academical, and Professional. As far as my acquaintance with American colleges and Universities extends, the ancient reproach of bigoted scholasticism has wholly passed away. The despotism of Aristotle and Plato; the slavish transmission from age to age of jejune systems; the trammels of a sterile logic, productive of nothing but verbal puzzles and controversial subtleties; the use of arid manuals, and of the learned languages, to the exclusion of the vernacular, as the vehicles of instruction; the neglect of modern and contemporary literature and natural and practical science; all these short-comings and prejudices and obstinate adherences to the past have, in the American colleges and in many of the European, past away. The leaning with us is rather to the other extreme; the too prompt and facile adoption of novelties in the modes and subjects of study, and in the objects and conduct of collegiate education. As far as my own observation has extended, the spirit of progress and improvement is as much alive at our places of education as in any of the walks of active life.

The branches of study usually pursued in our higher American seminaries, are mainly the following: 1. Languages, principally the ancient, but not excluding modern foreign languages and the philosophical study of our own; 2. Science, in its two great branches of exact and applied; 3. Physiology, in all its departments, meaning thereby the knowledge of external nature, animate and inanimate; 4. The philosophy of the mind, or the investigation of the intellectual powers; 5. History, the general record of human action and progress; 6. The various branches of social science, including civil polity, political economy, and constitutional law; 7. The circle of the moral sciences, comprehending all those which rest on the discrimination of right and wrong; and, 8. The relations and duties of man as a spiritual and religious being.*

It will probably be admitted that some acquaintance with most of these branches of knowledge, would be highly desirable as a preparation for almost any calling of active life. But it is the intention of the Trustees of the Washington University of the State of Missouri to give a peculiarly practical development and application to the studies designated under the second and third heads. To this end they propose to connect with the institution, as a prominent and peculiar feature in its

* The charter of the Washington University of the State of Missouri divests the institution of all sectarian or denominational character.

plan, departments for the useful and the fine arts, in which the youth of the West shall be furnished with such systematic instruction, as shall enable them to carry to the factory, to the laboratory, to the quarry, to the mine, and to the farm, that scientific knowledge which is required to deduce practice from theory; to give dignity as well as efficiency to labor; and connect abstract principles with the industrial pursuits of life. They feel that this mighty West requires an education, in some respects, of a peculiar character,—corresponding with its great extent, the unexampled rapidity of its growth, and the magnitude of all its relations, social, industrial, and political. While they are determined, as far as depends upon them, that its emulous young men shall enjoy all the advantages of academical education, in the best forms in which it is known in older communities, it is no less their fixed purpose to furnish the requisite scientific preparation for the intenser life that exists in the great valley of the Mississippi.

Such being the case, it would be surely a waste of time to undertake, on this occasion, and before this audience, a general vindication of university studies, against the imputation to which I have above referred, inasmuch as the greater part of the studies in all our American collegiate institutions have an evident and avowed tendency and design toward practical utility; and that end will be especially kept in view, in the institution whose establishment we this day inaugurate. I shall therefore, in the remainder of this discourse, confine myself to the inquiry, whether the unfavorable impression of which I have spoken is founded in reason or popular prejudice, in reference to those particular studies which are usually objected to as antiquated, scholastic, and abstract; such as language, and especially the dead languages; the higher mathematics; and metaphysics, as that branch is usually called. A few hints only on each topic are all that the limits of the occasion will permit.

1. And first language, which is sometimes disparaged by an invidious contrast between words and things; and the dead languages, so called I suppose by *antiphrasis*, because some of them have outlived ninety generations of our race, and in all human probability will outlive as many more. What then is this so much disparaged language? It is the sign and image, the embodiment, the incarnation (if I may presume to use the word) of this spiritual thing which we call thought, including in that term, for convenience, all the mental exercises. I will not insist, with some philosophers, that the *word*, written or spoken, is essential to the existence of the *idea*, though I cannot myself practically separate them. But if it were admitted that, in the secret recesses of the mind, there could be thoughts unassociated with words to represent them, still, it would be certain that without language, there could be no revelation of thought to the outer world. Here, then, let us pause for a moment, and, with the aid of this preliminary view, contemplate the sublime functions and the mysterious significance of language, as the representative of thought, and judge whether it is a subject worthy to engage our attention at a place of education.

This wonderful essence, then, which we call mind, of which thought is the exercise, which, under Providence, governs all created things subjected to man;

which moves material masses; guides and controls natural forces; develops and applies physical properties; gathers and regulates the societies of men; the created life of the universe, without which all else would be a senseless clod, an irrational machine, a body without a soul; this mind, I say,—essence mysterious, ineffable, sovereign;—where is it, what is it, how acts it? I cannot feel it, I cannot see it, I cannot hear it. It has no substance, no shape, no parts, no whole. It gives perception to the senses, but I cannot in turn perceive it; it is not sense. At its bidding, the valves of the heart permit the conscious blood to pour tumultuously into the blushing cheeks, or to rush back fainting and affrighted from their pallid collapsing cells; but it is not the heart nor the blood. It sends out living nerves from the lordly brain and the stately column that supports it, to the remotest avenues of feeling; but it is not brain or nerve. It hears with the ear and it sees with the eye, but it is not eye nor ear. It is every where within me but not any where, inscrutably wrapped up in this muddy vesture of decay, every particle of which it clothes with beauty, and life, and power.

How does this unseen and spiritual nature manifest and express itself; how does it act upon surrounding fellow-men, on kindred minds, in other regions, in after ages? It manifests itself, it becomes perceptible, it enters into communion with kindred mind, chiefly by the agency of articulate speech; by the twofold interchangeable mystery of language; this double system of intelligible signs; the one a few black marks addressed to the eye, the other delicate vocal undulations of the air addressed to the ear,—too faint to be perceived by the other senses ; totally different from each other, and both as different from the mind itself (which they represent) as matter and spirit ; and yet made by a standing miracle not only to express with automatic accuracy and electric speed the minutest shades of thought ; but to do it at pleasure in the language of the eye or the language of the ear, as if they were one and the same thing ; instead of being as radically distinct as sight and sound, or as air and light.

Such is language, the representative of thought. Dwell upon it, I pray you, a moment longer ; it is a great mystery of our being. By the use of a few written or printed lines on paper, so like each other, that, in languages with which we are unfamiliar,—witness a Malay or a Japanese manuscript,—there seems scarce any difference between them ; this unseen, intangible, mysterious mental essence, compared with which a perfume, a sound, a lunar rainbow is gross and material, expresses itself to the eye ; by the gentle impulse, the soft vibrations, which the lips impart to the elastic air it expresses itself to the ear. To give the spoken word duration, I translate it into written character ;—to give the written sign a vital emphasis, I translate it into vocal speech. By one divine art, the dead letter, charged with a living meaning, sounds through echoing halls, and wins or storms its way to sympathetic hearts ; by another, the fleeting wavelets of the air are crystallized into a most marvellous permanence, and become imperishable gems of thought, whose lustre no lapse of time can obscure ; while, by the union of both, this incomprehensible being, the mind, gently wooed from the vestal chambers of our inmost nature, comes forth like a bride adorned for her lordly spouse, the word; clad in the rich vesture of conversation, of argument, of eloquence, of poetry, of song; to walk with him the busy or the secluded paths of life; to instruct and delight the living generations; ethereal essences as they are, to outlive columns of brass and pyramids of granite; and to descend in eternal youth the unending highways of the ages.

Does it seem much that the skill of men has in these latter days contrived the means of communicating intelligence almost with the rapidity of thought, across the expanse of continents and beneath the depth of oceans by the electric wire? That a message despatched from Boston at midday, will so far out-travel the sun as to reach St. Louis an hour before he arrives at that meridian? It is much, and we contemplate with just amazement the wonderful apparatus which, when laid down, as sooner or later it perhaps will be, so as to connect the three continents, may, by possibility, send the beginning of such a sentence as I am now pronouncing around the terraqueous globe and return it to the lips of the speaker, before he has completed its utterance. But this amazing apparatus is but another form of language; it transmits intelligence only as it transmits words. It is like speech, like the pen, like the press, another piece of machinery by which language is conveyed from place to place. The really wonderful thing is language itself, by which thought is made sensible and communicated from mind to mind, not only in the great living congregation of the civilized world for the time being, but through the vast general assembly of the ages: by which we are able at this moment, not only to listen to all the great utterances which express the thoughts and emotions of the present day throughout the world, but to soar with Milton to the green fields of Paradise in the morning of creation; to descend with Dante to the depths of penal woe; to listen to the thunders of Tully and Demosthenes, and, by the golden chain of etymology, trace the affinity and descent of nations back, through the labyrinth of the past, almost to the cradle of the race.

I hold in my hand a portion of the identical electrical cable, given me by my friend, Mr. Peabody, which is now * in progress of manufacture, to connect America with Europe. I read upon it the following words: "A part of the submarine electric telegraph cable, manufactured by Messrs. Glass & Co. of London, for the Atlantic telegraph company, to connect St. Johns, Newfoundland, with Valencia, Ireland, a distance of sixteen hundred and forty nautical, or nineteen hundred statute miles." Does it seem all but incredible to you that intelligence should travel for two thousand miles, along those slender copper wires, far down in the all but fathomless Atlantic, never before penetrated by aught pertaining to humanity, save when some foundering vessel has plunged with her hapless company to the eternal silence and darkness of the abyss? Does it seem, I say, all but a miracle of art, that the thoughts of living men,—the thoughts that we think up here on the earth's surface in the cheerful light of day,—about the markets, and the exchanges, and the seasons, and the elections, and the treaties, and the wars, and all the fond nothings of daily life, should clothe themselves with elemental sparks, and shoot with fiery speed

* April 22, 1857.

in a moment, in the twinkling of an eye, from hemisphere to hemisphere, far down among the uncouth monsters that wallow in the nether seas, along the wreck-paved floor, through the oozy dungeons of the rayless deep;—that the last intelligence of the crops, whose dancing tassels will in a few months be coquetting with the westwind on these boundless prairies, should go flashing along the slimy decks of old sunken galleons, which have been rotting for ages; that messages of friendship and love, from warm living bosoms should burn over the cold green bones of men and women, whose hearts, once as warm as ours, burst as the eternal gulfs closed and roared over them, centuries ago?—Behold another phenomenon of a surety not less surprising,—an intellectual electrical telegraph,—if I may so call it,—not less marvellous! The little volume which I hold in my hand contains the two immortal poems of Homer, those world-renowned strains, which one of the imperial minds of our race, not far from thirty centuries ago, poured forth in the delighted ears of heroic Greece, while the softest down of youth was upon the cheek of its young nationality,—those glowing golden legends,—that sovereign wrath of Achilles, which

——— shall burn unquenchably,
Until the eternal doom shall be,—

the parting of Hector and Andromache,—a scene to which the sad experience of three thousand years could not add one image of tenderness and sorrow; the threats of Jupiter to the awe-struck gods, while every peak of Olympus was ablaze with his leaping thunders; the piteous supplications of aged Priam, kissing the hand and bathing with his tears the feet of the cruel chieftain, who had dragged the torn body of his noble son three times round the Ilian walls; the weary and sorrowful wanderings of Ulysses, which every subsequent age of mankind has retraced with delight,—these all, like the cunningly imprisoned airs of a musical box, breathe to us in one perennial strain of melody from within the covers of this small volume. By the simple agency of twenty-four little marks, stamped on the written or the printed page, the immortal legend has flashed down to us through the vicissitudes of empires and eras;—across the vast expanse of enlightened and benighted periods of history;—from region to region, from his own rocky islet in the Ægean to shores unknown, undreamed of, by him;—beneath the overwhelming billows of three thousand years, where peoples whole have sunk; and it now binds together, by the golden wires of intellect and taste, the mind of Europe and America, at this meridian of their refinement, with the mind of every intervening age of literary culture, back to the cradle of infant Greece. And while, at our places of education, we diligently investigate the wonderful properties of matter developed in the phenomena of the physical world, shall we not, my friends, deem a portion of our time and attention well bestowed upon the miracles of the *word*, written and spoken,—the phenomena of language, which lie at the foundation of all our intellectual improvement, of all our literature and science, in a word, of all rational communication between man and man?

2. The mathematics, abstract and applied, form another leading branch of study, especially as pursued in scientific and polytechnic schools; and one, I suppose, which the majority of young persons regard with least favor and

pursue with least success, either as attended in the higher departments of the study with greater difficulty,—or as requiring a peculiar aptitude possessed by fewer persons,—or as supposed to be less directly applicable to the business and duties of after-years. Beyond the little arithmetic required for the ordinary economies of life, the mass of college-bred men, unless engaged in the business of instruction or in pursuits which directly involve their application, from the time they leave their places of education, of whatever name, give up the Mathematics as a useless and hopeless abstraction.

But more closely viewed, the Mathematics, like language, (of which indeed they may be considered a species,) comprehending under that designation the whole science of number, space, form, time, and motion, as far as it can be expressed in abstract formulas, are evidently not only one of the most useful, but one of the grandest of studies. Commencing with arithmetic, which, however humble and familiar its processes, is the pivot on which the business of the world turns, either as regards private fortunes or the policies of great states; ascending through algebra and geometry, where lies the broad field of nearly all the applied sciences and many of the mechanical and manufacturing, and some even of the fine arts,—for music and drawing and architecture have their mathematical principles,—till we reach those transcendental refinements of the calculus by which the great dynamical problems of the Universe are solved and the laws of its phenomena demonstrated, it is evident that no other study can exceed the mathematics, not merely in the variety of their applications to the service of man, but in proper dignity and importance.

A large part of the training of the engineer, civil and military, as far as preparatory studies are concerned; of the builder of every fabric of wood, or stone, or metal, designed to stand upon the earth, or bridge the stream, or resist or float upon the wave; of the surveyor who lays out a building lot in a city, or runs a boundary line between powerful governments across a continent; of the geographer, navigator, hydrographer, and astronomer,—must be derived from the mathematics. Although with the majority of those who study and practice in these capacities, second-hand acquirements, trite formulas, and appropriate tables are sufficient for ordinary purposes, yet these trite formulas and familiar rules were originally or gradually deduced from the profound investigations of the most gifted minds, from the dawn of science to the present day. A most important case recently adjudicated in the East, has shown that the highest mathematical principles may be involved in the production of the simplest mechanical result. The further developments of the science, with its possible applications to larger purposes of human utility and grander theoretical generalizations, is an achievement reserved for a few of the choicest spirits, touched from time to time by Heaven to these highest issues. The intellectual world is filled with latent and undiscovered truth as the material world is filled with latent electricity. The latter, "much enforced" by our cylinders and batteries, "shows a hasty spark," which is straight reabsorbed into the surrounding medium; but the new truth, which is struck out from the all-surrounding realm of thought, will shine and burn, unabsorbed and unabsorbable, till the partial glimpses we now catch of the material universe shall kindle up into the broad effulgence, and the unclouded illumination, of higher spheres of being and knowledge.

But it would be a grievous wrong to mathematical, as indeed to any science, to rest its importance mainly on a utilitarian basis. The great truths with which it deals, are clothed with an austere grandeur, far above all purposes of immediate convenience or profit. It is in them that our limited understandings approach nearest to the conception of that absolute and infinite, toward which in most other things they aspire in vain. In the pure mathematics we contemplate absolute truths, which existed in the divine mind before the morning stars sang together, and which will continue to exist there, when the last of their radiant host shall have fallen from heaven. They existed not merely in metaphysical possibility, but in the actual contemplation of the supreme reason. The pen of inspiration, ranging all nature and life for imagery to set forth the Creator's power and wisdom, finds them best symbolized in the skill of the surveyor. "He meted out heaven as with a span;" and an ancient sage, neither falsely nor irreverently, ventured to say, that "God is a geometer." Yes, precisely by the same calculus by which I might number the individuals on this platform, has the Omniscient mind numbered the leaves in the interminable forest, the sands on the sea-shore, the particles of light that radiate from a universe of suns, the atoms of the ethereal medium, if such there be, which fills the infinite of space. The same divine enginery which shapes the drop now falling from my finger, gave its form to the unfathomable ocean which encompasses the globe, to the moon which heaves the weltering tides of that ocean from their darksome beds, to the sun which chains moon and earth alike to the eternal centre. The laws which keep that roof from falling on our heads, are no other than those which suspend the fluid ring of Saturn,—a bottomless and shoreless ocean, as it has been shown to be, by our own Bond and Peirce,—high in the heavens above the encircled planet, upheld in circumfluent equilibrium, by his eight sustaining moons. The teacher of the village school, who draws an ellipse on the blackboard, has described the curve of revolution of every luminary that travels the infinite of space. Those principles which are true in the recitation-room, are true in the nebula of Hercules; as true when they carry a falling apple to the earth, as when they wheel the starry universe about its central sun.

3. But not less important or interesting as a branch of university education than language or mathematics, is the philosophy of the mind, though somewhat discredited, it may be feared, under the accidental, and, as usually interpreted, not very significant name of metaphysics. If it be true that "the proper study of mankind is man," surely there is no part of that study so worthy of our attention as those intellectual powers,—the nature and functions of that spiritual essence,—in which man chiefly differs from the beasts that perish. In much that belongs to our material frames we share with them a common organization; nay, in those bodily senses and organs which belong to both, they sometimes excel us. The eagle discerns the sportsman from a greater distance than

the sportsman discerns the eagle. The antelope is fleeter of foot and quicker of ear than his pursuer. All that marvellous and inexplicable network of vein, and artery, and nerve, however various the detail of its structure, exists in the same astonishing complication in the subject animals, as in man.

But without attempting to define the nature, or assign the limits of the wonderful instincts, possessed by the humbler orders of sentient beings, we may safely claim an unshared preëminence for man, in the glorious prerogative of reasoning mind ; and the study of its mysterious powers and faculties, besides its practical utility for the purposes of education and mental discipline, is surely as noble an exercise of thought as can engage our time and attention.

It is true the inquiry is attended with peculiar difficulty, arising from the very circumstances which give it interest and importance. Clothed with material bodies, endowed with material organs and senses, and connected with our fellow-men and the world around us by material ties, not merely convenience and habit, but the very necessities of our being, direct our first attention to the outer world and give a paramount importance to material nature, in reference to all the ordinary business and duties of life. But outward nature and our material frames are a part only of our being. We are conscious of a spiritual essence within us, endued with a higher order of faculties, and destined, as we believe, to a higher sphere of life and action, when our bodily frames, and the vital relations in which we are placed by them, shall have passed away.

This transcendent mystery of our nature is the subject

of the philosophy of the mind. It rises from extension and solidity, and weight, and form, and color,—wonderful properties, I grant, of some wonderful, undiscovered, and probably undiscoverable substratum, which we call matter, to the incalculably higher properties of perception, attention, abstraction, association, imagination, memory ;—the exalted attributes of the intellectual nature. It seeks, through the careful study of their operations, and a patient scrutiny of our own consciousness, to acquire some accurate knowledge of these exalted powers ; of that *intuition* which darts to its goal more swiftly than the electric spark to the completion of its circuit ; of that *abstraction* which gathers from a thousand actual existences the common attributes which are concrete in all, and separate in none; of that *association* which binds our ideas in chains as strong as they are often mysterious and arbitrary ; of that *imagination* which neither space, nor time, nor nature can limit ; of that *memory* which gives continuity to our intellectual being, and preserves the sacred deposit of a life of action and thought ; of those *emotions* and *passions* which impart to character its force ; of that *will* which determines the moral character of our actions ; of that *conscience* which reigns supreme over the whole realm of voluntary and responsible conduct.

Can we doubt the dignity and importance of such a study ? Shall we think it a profitable employment of time to devote weeks, and months, and years to the investigation of the circulatory system of the poor beetle that frets the velvet cheek of the rose-bud ; to the discovery of the periods of binary stars, whose separate existence as faint sparks of light in the remotest heavens can only be detected by telescopes of the highest defining power; to the assignment of the geological age of strange trilobites, and paradoxical fish-lizards, that ceased to exist uncounted ages before the present orders of being on earth began, but which the science of these latter days has evoked from the marble jaws of her lowest strata,—shall objects like these occupy our time and deserve our attention, as I admit they do, for the hand of the Creator is as visible in them all,—in the star, the fossil, and the insect, as in the sun which it guided this morning from the horizon to the zenith,—and shall we find no interest in the inquiry into the nature of the very faculties by which we conduct these curious investigations, and contrive the marvellous apparatus by which they are pursued; which enable the sagacious, the patient, the ardent lover of truth, to work the miracles of inductive reasoning; which embolden him, not with presumptuous daring but with reverential aspiration, to build the sublime stories of analogy to the highest heaven; * to pierce the earth almost to its core; to achieve those triumphs of invention and demonstration, of art and of science, in which our frail nature makes its nearest approach to the infinite and the divine.

I know it is objected to the study of the philosophy of the mind, that all our labor and research must end with the inquiry into the *operation* of the mental powers, and that it is impossible to penetrate to the mental *essence*. But, great heavens, is not this equally the case with the study of matter? Do not all our labor, and all our research in the study of nature, end with the discovery of

* Amos, ix. 6.

material properties; and is it not equally impossible to penetrate to material essence? Are not extension, solidity, form, temperature, color, ductility, elasticity, magnetism, electricity, and gravitation, the master quality of all,—mere properties, primary or secondary, of the unknown, hidden basis which we call matter; and which defies alike the piercing eye of the microscope, the merciless search of the crucible, the biting tooth of the solvent acid, and the all-subduing, blasting energy of the voltaic spark. It may be burned to ashes, or ground to powder, or melted to glass, or evaporated into air, and not a ray of light will be thrown upon its nature. The all-wise Creator has placed the bars and the bolts of impenetrable mystery as firmly on the secret nature of the material as of the immaterial world. We know them both but in their properties and qualities. In what those properties inhere we are in both cases profoundly and equally ignorant; and it is the great superiority of the intellectual nature, that it is endowed with those faculties, by which alone, not merely the wonders of its own consciousness, but all the phenomena of the outer world are explored and comprehended.

These natural sciences, as we call them, are but logical sequences of thought;—these branches of physical knowledge are the creations of intellect. The celestial vault sparkling with its countless suns is but a darkling blank, till the sun of reason,—the immortal mind,—has shot a perceptive glance up to its peerless glories. The brightest star has no eye to behold its own lustre or that of its sister star. This infinite loveliness of nature on earth holds no mirror up to itself; the prairie has no eye for the flowers that paint it; the forest has no ear for the crashing symphonies of the whirlwind. The river rolls along unconscious of its verdant bank;—the verdant bank drinks in no music from the murmuring stream. This gorgeous atmospheric drapery, which hangs its aerial festoons over land and sea, lined at morning and eventide with cloudy lutestrings of purple and gold, and dipped at noon in ultrameridian blue; these columnar mountains, whose granitic architraves, carved and fretted with the tempests of ages, support the vaulted sky; these great arterial rivers which drain the waters of whole continents into the mighty ocean alembic, thence to be carried by vaporous distillation to the piteous heavens, to be wept down again in compassionate showers upon the parched earth;—this heavenly concert of falling waters, and sighing breeze, and rustling grove, vocal with all the music of spring,—were lost, but for the human intellect. There is in all creation, below God and the angels, no eye for the beauty, no ear for the melody, no sense for the fragrance, no perception for the symmetry, no comprehension for the unutterable bounty, dignity, and grandeur, but in the rational mind. It would all lie hushed, and blank, and cold, but for the vitality enkindled in it from the living sense of intelligent man. I pass by, at this time, as too vast, too various even for the most hasty enumeration, the novel forms and wondrous combinations wrought in the natural elements by the inventive and disposing powers of mind; as I do also of necessity the intellectual and moral creations of our reasoning and imaginative faculties.

Yes, my friends, this external creation is unutterably magnificent and fair; but we have "that *within* which passeth show." Not all the kingdoms of the earth, with all their wonders, which the lying tempter promised to the patient Son of God from that exceeding high mountain to which he had taken him up, can be compared to the wonders of the little world within; of that creative principle through which and by which alone the power, and wealth, and grace of the material world are perceived and explored. I repeat it, the phenomena of matter exist for us, only as they are disclosed by the contemplations of mind. Is it not so? Trace the history of science from its commencement. Since the world began, the magnetic attraction had dwelt uncomprehended beneath its flickering auroral canopy enthroned "on the sides of the North;" traversing unobserved the curve of its inscrutable oscillations, and breathing its unperceived influence all round the globe. The acuteness of some happy observer in what we arrogantly call the dark ages, (the ages that built cathedrals, and taught their arches to resound to organs attuned to the praises of the Most High,—which produced the Divina Commedia and the Canterbury Tales,) penetrated the outer vestibule of this elemental mystery; and—oh, divine compensation,—from behind the eternal battlements of this ice-bound unapproachable North, from within those frozen portals, where even now the hardiest frames and the stoutest hearts knock for admittance,—in vain, alas, as the recent sorrows of the whole country too well attest,—went forth the guiding spirit, the trembling little pilot which conducts the mariner over the pathless ocean, beneath the darkest night, to the uttermost ends of the earth. Since the world began, the vapor of heated water had risen, and diffused, and lost itself in the air; ages on ages passed by and witnessed unconsciously this stupendous waste of mechanical power; till the keen reflection, the patient research, the untiring perseverance of a long line of philosophers, ending in Watt and Fulton, grappled with the problem, and brought to perfection the machinery which has turned these fleeting watery atoms into a mighty mechanical force, revolutionized the industrial world, and for all the purposes of material power has, within the last half century, doubled the population of the globe. Since the world began, the lightning had played harmlessly upon the fringes of the distant cloud, or shot its three-bolted artillery in dreadful volleys through the piled and rolling embrasures of the storm, till a creative glance of Franklin's mind, just a hundred years ago this year, pierced the hidden nature of the subtle element, and laid the foundation of those discoveries which have been since made the instrument of transmitting that thought which it most resembles across continents and oceans, and recording the movements of the furthest stars. Finally, the great frame of nature, from the infinitesimal molecule to the entire compacted universe, is held together by the law of gravity; every mote that floats in the sunbeam, every leaf that falls in the forest, every drop that distils from the clouds, every planet that encircles the sun, every sun which holds together its attendant system, and every system which swings in vast gyration through the infinite of space, obeys this mysterious power. But the sovereign law, though impressed on every particle of created matter, was written in hieroglyphics which Pythagoras, and Aristotle, and Archimedes, and Copernicus, and Keppler, and Galileo, and Bacon, beheld but could not decipher; and to which, at length, the mind of Newton first found the key, not two centuries ago.

No, my friends, when you make provision at your places of education for the study of the philosophy of the mind, it is no refined abstraction or scholastic subtlety to which you invite the student's attention. You seek to impart to him the knowledge of that principle within us, whose essence indeed is inscrutable, but whose faculties, under providence, rule with divine vicegerency the created world, and stamp upon our frail humanity the reflected image of the Creator. Yes, noble Aristotle, thou or thy commentators are right. *Μετὰ τὰ φυσικά* this divine philosophy may well be called;—after—beyond the natural things. The region to which the philosophy of the mind conducts us, dimly discerned in the present state of being, lies far off, beyond the realms of material nature; beyond these crowded cities, and fertile fields, and dewy vales, where some of us linger with sobered step, and the youngest of you, my friends, will soon reach the goal; beyond the lofty hills that bound the horizon, and which fly before us as we advance; over the land and over the sea; broader than earth, and ocean, and sky; above these burning stars which speak down to us in the still watches of night, from the sacred heavens; behind these veils of aching, fainting, dying flesh. After the bloom of the cheek has faded; after the wreath of fame has withered; after the taste of pleasure has palled ; after nature, after time, after life, after death, we reach at last the pleasant land,

> " Sweet fields beyond the rolling flood,"—

where the philosophy of the mind awaits, at the foot of the Cross, from a WISDOM higher than its own, the complete solution of its momentous problems.

Go on, then, my friends, in your praiseworthy undertaking. The cause in which you are engaged is that of civilization, of virtue, of truth, and of religion. The influences you seek to strengthen and extend are those, which in three centuries have brought our beloved America from the infancy of barbarism to her honorable position in the family of nations. The studies for which you make provision are not only the skilful purveyors to the common wants of our nature, but the ministers to its purest delights. The faculties you endeavor to discipline and to cultivate, are those which raise intellectual man above the savage and the brute. Complete then your already liberal endowments. Fill your departments with able and faithful instructors. Establish on a permanent basis a liberal seminary of education ; a great school of literature, science, and the arts. Collect an ample library—that great, silent, but all-eloquent teacher of every branch of knowledge. Found an observatory* upon the meridian of St. Louis, the ninetieth west from Greenwich, and thereby admirably adapted for the comparison of observations. Let solid learning, and sound principle, and pure morals go

* See Appendix, B.

forth to the rising West, from this, one of the chief *foci* of her natural communications and expanding commerce. Your honored fellow-citizen, Judge BATES, has just compared it to the spider's web, which gathers to its centre whatever ventures within its circuit; let it be also a genial sun, sending forth its beams of light and truth to the farthest bounds of this imperial valley. Be faithful to the great heritage of freedom, prosperity, and power which you have received from your fathers. Enter into a generous emulation with your older sister States, and thus keep alive the kindly sympathies which bind the cultivated mind of the country together. In your day of small things, remember the infancy of those "twins of learning" in the East; the frugal legacy that gave being to Harvard, the few precious volumes that founded Yale; not doubting that the time will come, if your enlightened views shall be shared by your successors, that the seminary you are now founding will take rank hereafter with those venerable patriarchs of our literary republic. The dust of your fathers, with few exceptions, lies side by side with the dust of our fathers in the honored soil of the East. On that soil—may the love of Heaven forever fall in gentle dews upon it—many of yourselves first drew the breath of life. Let these tender associations give strength to the sacred bond of brotherhood which unites us, and before the dark day shall arrive that witnesses its rupture, may these eyes be closed beneath the sod. Above all, my friends, lay the corner-stone of your institution on the Rock of Ages, and may the blessing of Heaven rest upon it.

APPENDIX.

A.

The change in the Charter, above indicated, was made by the insertion of the following sections, in compliance with the petition of the Directors to the General Assembly of Missouri. [Act approved February 12, 1857.]

Sec. 2. No instruction, either sectarian in religion, or party in politics, shall be allowed in any department of said University, and no sectarian or party test shall be allowed in the election of professors, teachers, or other officers of said University, or in the admission of scholars thereto, or for any purpose whatever.

Sec. 3. It shall be the duty of the Board of Directors of said University, upon being informed of any violation of the second section of this act, forthwith to institute an inquiry into the charge or charges that may be preferred in respect thereof, by any credible person, in writing, against any officer of said University; and if it shall appear that any officer of said University has violated the said second section of this act, the Board of Directors shall forthwith remove such person so offending, from any office which he may then fill in any department of said University; and such person so removed shall be forever thereafter ineligible to any office in said University.

Sec. 4. In case the Board of Directors, upon being notified in writing by any credible person of a violation of the second section of this act, shall refuse or neglect to investigate the charge hereupon preferred against any officer of said University, it shall be competent for the St. Louis Circuit Court, or the St. Louis Court of Common Pleas, to compel the Board of Directors, by *mandamus,* to perform their duty in investigating such charge, and to show their performance of such duty to the satisfaction of the court having cognizance of the matter; and all proceedings under this section shall be summary, and conducted to a conclusion with as little delay as possible; and the power hereby given to said courts may be exercised by the judge of either of said tribunals in vacation.

B.

THE Board of Directors are gratified to state that this appeal has met with a hearty and generous response from one of their own number. JAMES H. LUCAS, Esq., one of the most highly respected citizens of St. Louis, and to whose enterprise much of its prosperity is due, has declared his intention of building and endowing an Observatory, on a large and national scale, at an estimated cost of two hundred thousand dollars. For a work of such magnitude several years will, of course, be requisite, in order to its successful completion, but a beginning will be made at the earliest day practicable.

It is an interesting coincidence that Sir ISAAC NEWTON was *Lucasian* Professor of Mathematics. No better augury could be desired in the establishment of the LUCAS OBSERVATORY OF ST. LOUIS.

The Observatory buildings will not be erected on land now belonging to the University. A beautiful and commanding site containing twenty acres, has been set apart for the purpose by Mr. LUCAS, and will be used, unless some more suitable place can be found.

www.ingramcontent.com/pod-product-compliance
Lightning Source LLC
LaVergne TN
LVHW021430110826
845150LV00007B/2173
* 9 7 8 1 4 2 5 5 0 6 8 2 7 *